TO IDI AMIN
I'M A
IDIOT

and Other Palindromes

Also by Fred Yannantuono

A Boilermaker for the Lady (NYQ Books, 2009)

TO IDI AMIN
I'M A
IDIOT

and Other Palindromes

Fred Yannantuono

with illustrations by
Philippe Petit-Roulet

The New York Quarterly Foundation, Inc.
New York, New York

NYQ Books™ is an imprint of The New York Quarterly Foundation, Inc.

The New York Quarterly Foundation, Inc.
P. O. Box 2015
Old Chelsea Station
New York, NY 10113

www.nyq.org

Copyright © 2016 by Fred Yannantuono

Illustrations © 2016 by Philippe Petit-Roulet

All rights reserved. No part of this book may be used or reproduced in any manner whatsoever without written permission of the author except in the case of brief quotations embodied in critical articles and reviews.

First Edition

Set in New Baskerville

Layout and Design by Christina Sinibaldi
Cover Illustration by Philippe Petit-Roulet

Library of Congress Control Number: 2015901001

ISBN: 978-1-935520-90-0

TO IDI AMIN
I'M A
IDIOT

and Other Palindromes

Acknowledgments

A Boilermaker for the Lady	"Ugandan Palindrome"
Compass Rose	"More Amontillado Palindrome"
descant	"Tape to Tape Palindrome"
Eureka Literary Magazine	"Palindrome for an Average Player"
First Literary Review East	"Bureaucracy Palindrome," "Meditation Palindrome," "Reagan Palindrome," "Stripper's Wish List Palindrome"
Fugue	"Leeward Palindrome"
Light Quarterly	"Beautiful Dreamer Palindrome," "Creditor's Palindrome," "East Meets West Palindrome," "Halcyon Palindrome," "Instructions to a Masseuse Palindrome," "Melba is Toast Palindrome," "Message in a Bottle Palindrome," "Nightcap Palindrome," "Palindrome for a Bad Waitress," "Victoria's Secret Palindrome"
Lilies & Cannonballs	"Jaded Voyeur Palindrome"
New York Quarterly	"Canine Delusions of Grandeur Palindrome," "Canine Mistake Palindrome," "Chic Lit Palindrome," "An Exaltation of Hounds Palindrome," "Existential Book Choice Palindrome," "Icarus Palindrome," "Incest Palindrome," "Jewish Christmas Palindrome," "Magritte's Palindrome," "Mrs. Xerxes' Problem Palindrome," "On the 6th Day," "Sophisticated Courtship Palindrome"
New York Sun	"Cicada Plague Palindrome"
Poet Lore	"Metrical Sesame Palindrome"
Puerto Del Sol	"Axiomatic Palindrome"
Reflections	"How Rumors Spread Palindrome"
Rio Grande Review	"Nanny's Complaint Palindrome"

Contents

Leeward Palindrome   / 11
Palindrome for an Average Player   / 12
Halcyon Palindrome   / 15
Victoria's Secret Palindrome   / 16
Tape to Tape Palindrome   / 19
Icarus Palindrome   / 21
Palindrome for a Bad Waitress   / 22
Nanny's Complaint Palindrome   / 24
Metrical Sesame Palindrome   / 26
How Rumors Spread Palindrome   / 29
Message in a Bottle Palindrome   / 30
Elmer Fudd in Carnegie Hall Palindrome   / 32
Mrs. Xerxe's Problem Palindrome   / 35
Brian Epstein Palindrome   / 36
Incest Palindrome   / 38
We Really Like Ike Palindrome   / 40
Existential Book Choice Palindrome   / 42
Cowboy Requirement Palindrome   / 45
Bad Place to Crash Land Palindrome   / 46
Male Spider Palindrome   / 49
Where's Waldo Palindrome   / 50
Beautiful Dreamer Palindrome   / 53
Cicada Plague Palindrome   / 54
More Amontillado Palindrome   / 56
Montana Palindrome   / 58

Magritte's Palindrome   / 61
Should We Test for Tsetses Palindrome   / 62
On the Sixth Day Palindrome   / 64
Alfalfa's Birthplace Palindrome   / 66
Gay Serviceman Palindrome   / 69
Alcoholic's Fear Palindrome   / 70
Oliver Twist Palindrome   / 73
Melba is Toast Palindrome   / 74
Stripper's Wish List Palindrome   / 77
Meditation Palindrome   / 79
East Meets West Palindrome   / 81
Josephine's Palindrome   / 82
Typecasting Palindrome   / 85
Ethical Dilemma Palindrome   / 87
Bureaucracy Palindrome   / 88
Everything's Relative Palindrome   / 90

This book is affectionately dedicated to Sarah and Michael Palin, not necessarily in that order.

Way alee few do go ere, O God, we feel a yaw.

What are palindromes? Palindromes were invented by Michael Palin in 1967 as part of Monty Python's lumberjack skit, which reads the same forward and backward. The German version is palindromical too. Palin's rugby pals, *Otto* and *Bob*; his rare, giant Chihuahuas, *Anna, Nan,* and *Rotor;* and the rock band *ABBA* are legendary for the encouragement they provided. Still confused? *1) Amore, Roma; 2) I, Ed, sung an Agnus Dei;* and *3) To Oslo off? O no, it's a bastion of fools. Oot!* are palindromes too.

LEEWARD PALINDROME

PALINDROME FOR AN AVERAGE PLAYER

Tennis.
A lob? A rap?
O, no.
Parabolas
in net.

Studies suggest that tennis players are more adept at palindromes than their counterparts in football or golf. Bjorn Borg, for instance, wrote most of his award-winning palindromes while playing John McEnroe, having ample time during McEnroe's tantrums to put the finishing touches on work such as *1) Bold, low old lob. 2) Draw. Tendonitis is it. I nod netward. 3) Flog golf. 4) God damn as it ran alla breve: no, never ball an artisan, mad dog!*

'Twas Poseidon's nod. I, Esop, saw't.

Pose, Esop! Poseidon would cry, but Esop, knowing when to nod and when to acquiesce, would fire back *O not Alpha! Emit a gem or Omega! Time? Ah, Plato, no!*

HALCYON PALINDROME

VICTORIA'S SECRET PALINDROME

Desire cerulean E-cup? Puce? Nae, lure cerise D.

The perfect symmetry of the brassiere is paralleled in the form and content of the palindrome. Studies have shown that many people buying brassieres reflexively mouth phrases such as *O, no!* and *Tit!* while trying one on. Palin's gynecologist (he's a hypochondriac) routinely says things like *Tit. Left. Felt it.* The cortical areas a minimum of four inches from the cerebellum are believed to play a role in this process. Indeed, many lobotomized Americans have lost their abilities both to purchase brassieres and to construct even the most rudimentary of palindromes.

No, we were never ever even ere we won.

A palindrophilic tobogganist might be inspired to say *Si, 'tis a tie, but I tube it as it is.* Or *Tie? Yeah? Ha! Eye it!*

TAPE TO TAPE PALINDROME

Ho hum.
Uh oh!

Want to write a palindrome? Try this simple test. Does it read the same from right to left as left to right? Does it make sense? If so, you've written a palindrome. As to length, theorists have wrangled for decades about just how short a palindrome can be. Epidemiological studies suggest that Icarus was most likely just under four feet tall. Of course, the impact with the water may have compressed him slightly, but as Homer famously remarked, "Daddy knows what's Bosporus."

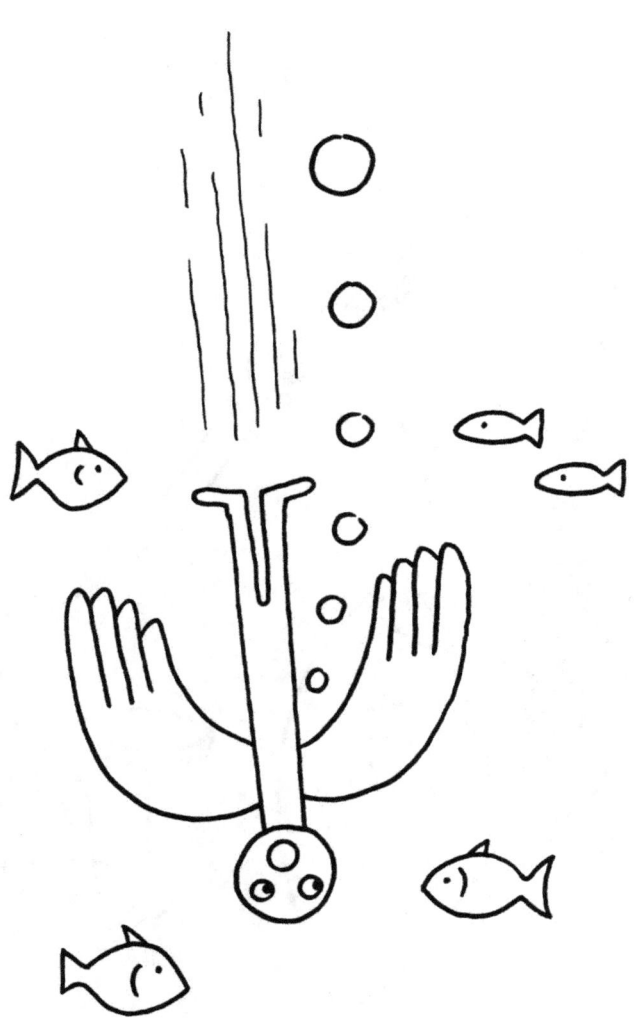

ICARUS PALINDROME

PALINDROME FOR A BAD WAITRESS

Lagniappe?*
You?
O, yep?—
Pain, gal!

*Louisiana French—tip, gratuity.
Waitresses are always coming and going…mostly named *Anna* or *Ava* or *Eve*.

NANNY'S COMPLAINT PALINDROME

Peel? Sew? Hell, it's drib drab rot: a gill, an alligator, Bard, birds, till, eh, we sleep.

From Shakespeare to Palin, a span of 360 years, the evolution of pre-palindromic forms continued apace. *To be or not to be botton roe bot,* the shadmonger's ubiquitous hawking cry along the Thames, was tragically shortened by Shakespeare to its current, unsophisticated form. Nevertheless, it was an early and unsuccessful flirtation between the Bard and this undiscovered mistress.

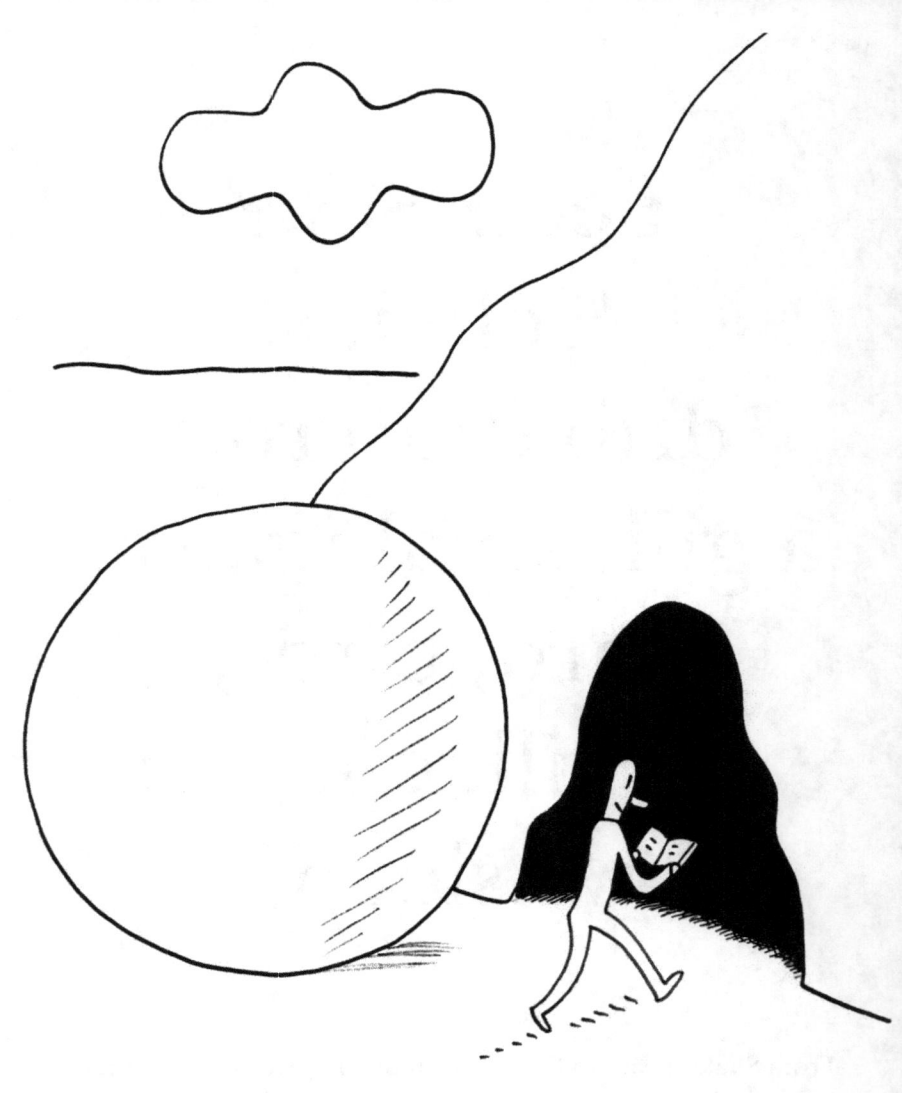

METRICAL SESAME PALINDROME

One poem, you buoy me. Open! O!

It's a little known fact that Shakespeare, the great sonneteer, once penned an instructional tract entitled *Sonnet: Ten No's*.

Idiot to idiot to idiot to idiot to idiot to idi...

It is rumored, though unsubstantiated, that one has to be, well, challenged to write palindromes, the theory being that a sophisticated mind is eager to get on with things and has an ingrained aversion to doubling back on itself whether for diversion, out of fatigue, or for paronomastic endeavors. Palin himself, as innovator, was the exception. His heirs and consigns, though, are by and large less discriminating. *Old? Well! Lil' Lord Avon as a Casanova? Droll I'll, lewd, lo!*

HOW RUMORS SPREAD PALINDROME

MESSAGE IN A BOTTLE PALINDROME

Tortuga's murder. Heave ho! Tosspots parted it. Pirates! Yo! Ha! Avast! It's Ava! Ahoy! Set a riptide trap. Stops sot. Oh Eva, eh? Red rum's a gut-rot.

Computer-generated palindromes have been known to go on for pages. They make no sense. A general rule of thumb is that, the longer the palindrome, the more likely it is that the second half is politically conservative, whereas the first half is radically leftist.

ELMER FUDD IN CARNEGIE HALL PALINDROME

He pways not tuba, nor, O moron, a button's yawp, eh?

Once, while driving through Rhode Island, Bugsy heard Elmer say, "*Did I cut a cwap 'n Pawcatuc? I did.*" From that point on he called him *Suo Fudd Dufous*. Yet Elmer also managed to pen, *Do I rail, O limed sun, even if I made Borodin a bared nude? No, it is opera repositioned under a ban I do robed. Am I fine, Venus de Milo? Liar! I OD*. Later in life, imprisoned in a tuba by Daffy, he composed the above.

Sex re Xerxes.

After all, she knew him well, and informed her purported beau, Edexes, *Tis sex, Ed. Exes sit,* to which he dubiously replied *Nae, copasetic sexes cite sap ocean.*

MRS. XERXES'S PROBLEM PALINDROME

BRIAN EPSTEIN PALINDROME

Yoko Ono ok? Oy!

Yoko Ono cut her eyeteeth protesting the palindromical Pythons, yet she once put a ladder up to a hole in a ceiling through which could be seen a small sign hand-lettered in script, reading, *Oedipus is up ideo.* Epstein, meanwhile, on a Christmas trip to Manhattan, blurted out when he first saw Central Park, *Go Jews! We jog!* Then *Yo Ho Ho! Oh, Oh. Oy!*

INCEST PALINDROME

Dad's eye, Mom's eye, Sis's eye eyes Sis, eyes Mom, eyes Dad.

Creon's manservant once said, *Aha! He no git'n Antigone. Ha. Ha.*

WE REALLY LIKE IKE PALINDROME

We kiss Ike. We kiss Ike. We kiss Ike. W...

Eisenhower employed a team of palindromists in the State Department. Nixon was piqued by their interoffice memo:
We emit Nixon: an ox in time. Ew!

EXISTENTIAL BOOK CHOICE PALINDROME

Hah! Sartre livres retro? Or terser, viler trash? Ah?

Sartre once, while visiting Camus, noticed a rash on Camus' arm. *Sumac, Camus?* Sartre asked pointedly. Camus replied poetically *Sumac flower: I fall as all afire, wolf Camus.*

To lasso hoss a lot.

Who has more time on his hands than a cowboy? At the end of a long day a herdin' 'n a ropin' 'n a brandin', what better way to unwind than to pistol whip a few bean-induced palindromes out of yourself like: *1) Ports o' Texas is axe to strop. 2) O maladroit? I or d'Alamo. 3) Free Jesse James. Sass 'em a Jesse jeer. Free Jesse James. Sass 'em a Jesse jeer. F.... 4) Bank nab. 5) On oot, tipsy spittoon, O! 6) No Omaha moon. 7) Nevada Dave 'n 8) Hey y'all, liter alcohol? Oho! Claret I'll lay yeh.*

COWBOY REQUIREMENT PALINDROME

BAD PLACE TO CRASH LAND PALINDROME

Splat! Alps.

"Beyond the Alps lie more Alps, and the Lord Alps those that Alps themselves," said Groucho, adding *'Tis Gummo. Mom mugs it.*

Deflowered ere wolfed.

Pity the poor male spider, although it's said the female's post-coital cannibalism leads to stronger offspring. Pythons eat spiders too, whose dying words, *Borp! Lair, O tan re bugaboo boob, a gubernatorial prob,* showcase the complexity of the issue.

MALE SPIDER PALINDROME

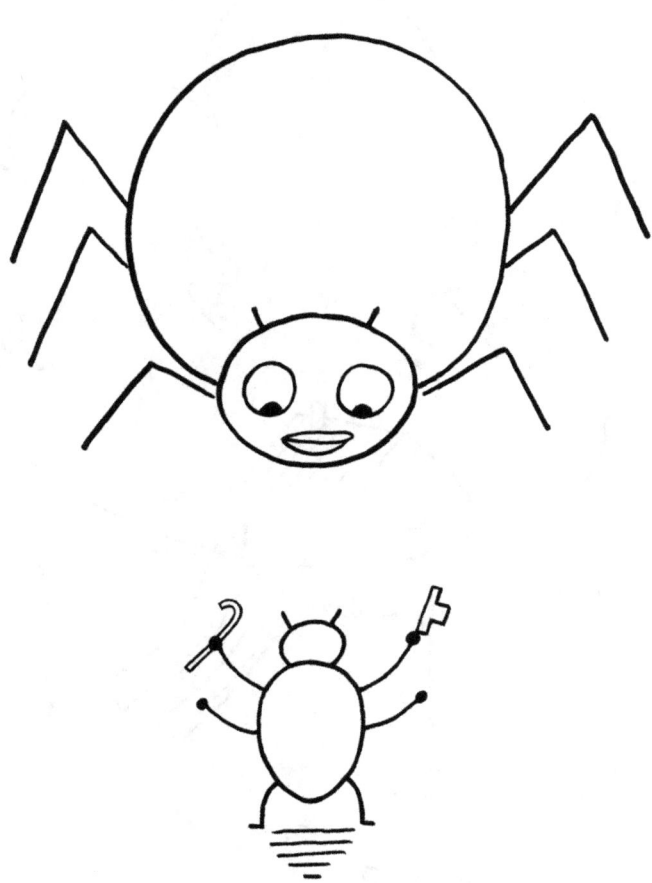

WHERE'S WALDO PALINDROME

Woodlawn, Waldo. Ow!

No palindrome has ever been penned in Woodlawn. Riverdale, on the other hand, along with Walla Walla, Washington—*He laid on all a Walla Walla call—a Walla Walla no dial, eh?*—is replete with such creations.

REMs, Em? I'm a reverie heir ever. Am I Mesmer?

Idolized by his associates, Mesmer was exceedingly modest. When extolled for his scientific epiphanies, he knocked ash from his meerschaum and replied *Epiphany? Nah. Pipe.*

BEAUTIFUL DREAMER PALINDROME

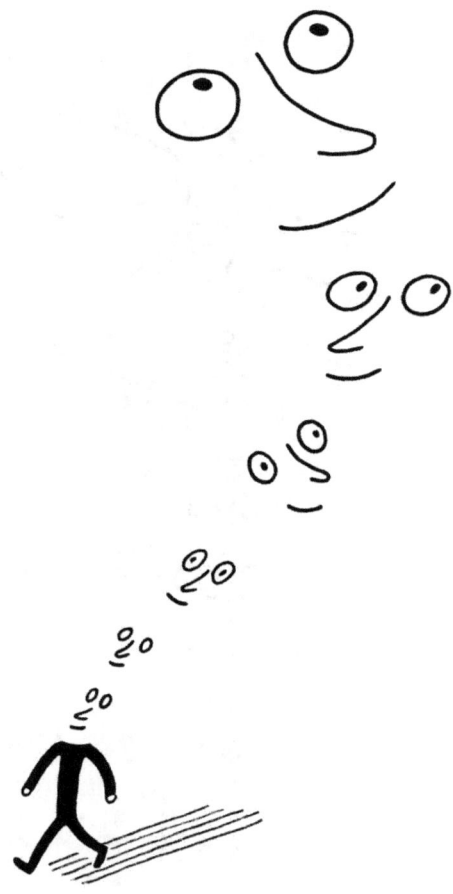

CICADA PLAGUE PALINDROME

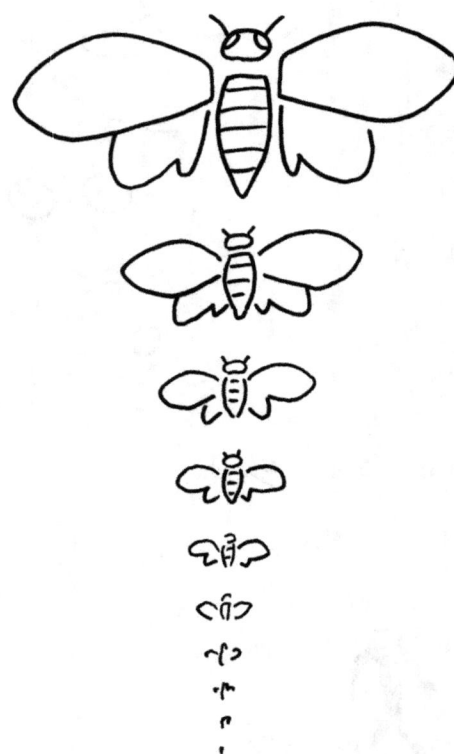

Cicada had a cicada had a cicada had a cicada had a cic…

Diogenes advanced the theories that insects themselves are palindromic. A caterpillar can invert its cephalic positioning. Bees fly backward. Thrips are gravitationally indulgent.

MORE AMONTILLADO PALINDROME

Hell, it's de trop, miss, as one taps reviled port, amontillado. God, all it—nom à—trop de livers, pâté. No sass! Imported still, eh?

The temerity of some palindromes: *Temerity, tire me, temerity, tire me, t...*Edgar Allan Poe's dentition indicates that he was both left and right handed. Bilingual palindromes like the above are illegal in most northern European countries, including Norway. Hence the everyday Norwegian expression *Trykk "Ga til bestilling" for a kjope reise med valgt reisedato tades iertglav demesi erep ojka rof gnillit sebli tagkk yrt.*

MONTANA PALINDROME

Et tu, Butte?

Montanans are notorious for their unalterable sense of place. A Montanan migrating to Alaska would inspire the dismissive: *Ha! He Montana man at Nome. Hah!*

Il a Dada, mon ami, no? T. S. Eliot is a tomato. My my! Mot à mot! As I toilest on I'm a nomad, a Dali.

"You don't write palindromes, you mine them," Palin has stated. "Like when you *mine denim*. They're in the language—anyone can find them, even you. While it may seem harder to write a bi-lingual palindrome, it's actually easier. When you run out of room in one language, if you can slop over into a second one, you've still got a shot at it. *Won't farceurs rue craft now?*"

MAGRITTE'S PALINDROME

SHOULD WE TEST FOR TSETSES PALINDROME

Tsetse? Yada yada yada. Yes, test.

Sleeping sickness can really wake one up. Remembering that diagnostically *Tsetse domesticity tic: I tse modes test,* and ignoring a doctor's *Tony, asset am I, tse tse pest! (Estimates say not)* could be precarious.

ON THE SIXTH DAY PALINDROME

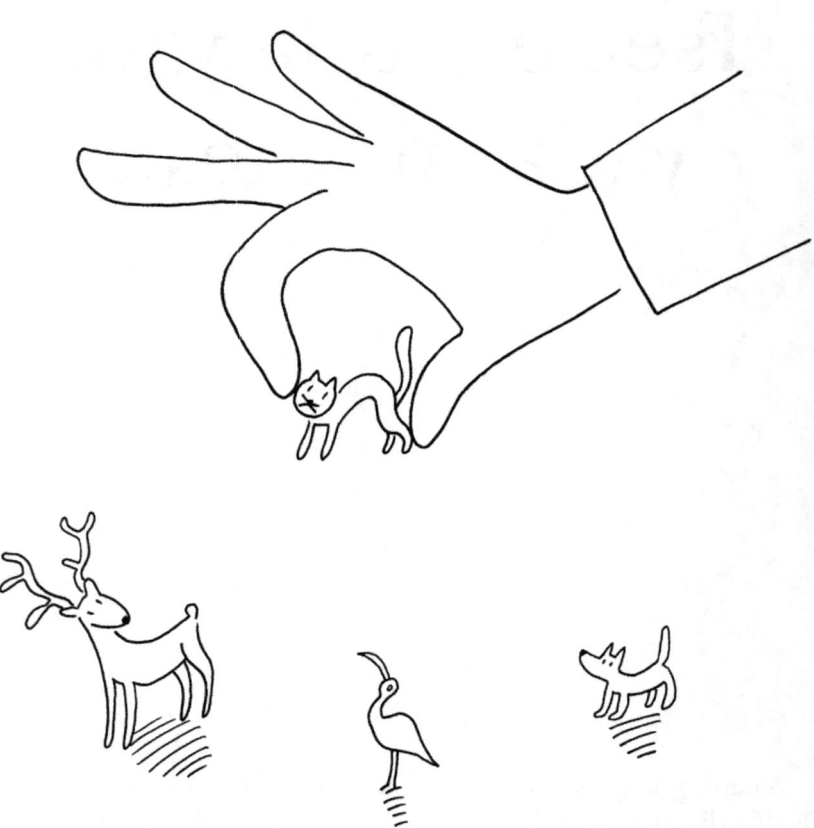

God tackles ibis, elk, cat, dog.

Of course your dog's reply to this might well be *Dog? I? Me?— Demigod!* or *A dog at apotheosis is, O, eh, to pat a God. A dog at apotheosis is, O, eh, to pat a God. A….* Time marches on and we all know that *animals ooze zoo's lamina*. Perhaps there's a lesson in this dreaming in reverse. Perhaps in Palin's dream of his poodle addressing him: *A hoot? God's rot: canaille. Well, I an actor's dog too. Ha!* or even *Dog doo? Good God!*

ALFALFA'S BIRTHPLACE PALINDROME

Alfalfa? Fla? Fla?

Wrong. Born in Paris, Illinois, even Alfalfa's doctor spoke French. His catch phrase? *En ici de medicine.*

Marine men I ram.

Homosexuality, when seen as a way to get from point A to point B and back again, is endemic to palindromy. It is estimated that up to 95% of palindromists are homosexual, bi-sexual, transsexual, transvesticitic, hermaphroditic, or heterosexual. *My nom? Oh, a homonym.* The remaining 5% are unfathomable. *Not a baton's not a baton.*

GAY SERVICEMAN PALINDROME

ALCOHOLIC'S FEAR PALINDROME

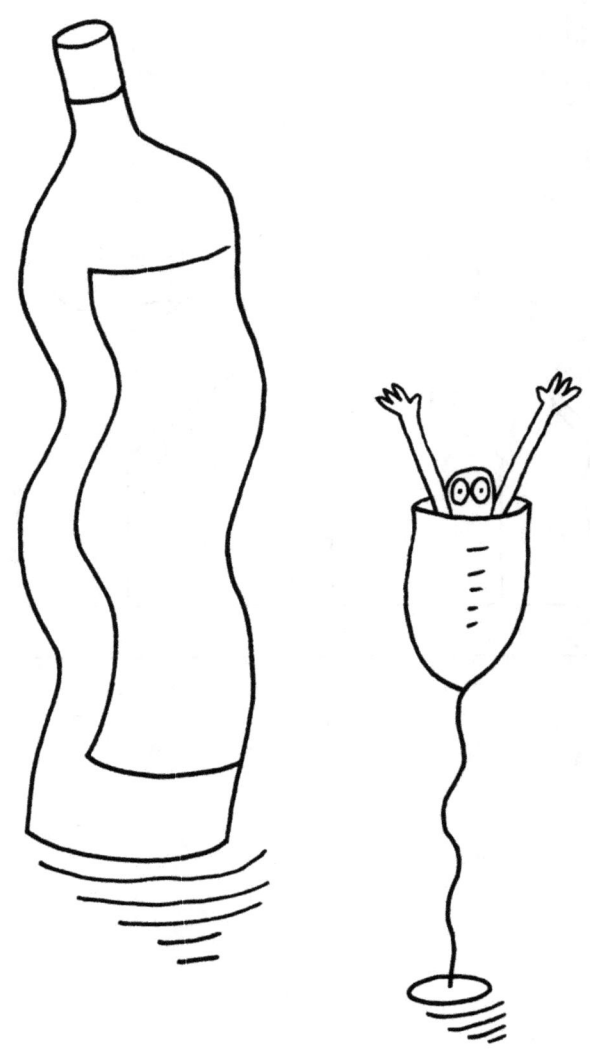

An amaretto to totter a man. An amaretto to totter a man. An amaretto to totter a man. A....

The ingestion of rum *(Rum! Rum's murmur!)* has never proved an effective tool in the writing of palindromes. On the other hand, the judgment of control groups could be called into question since none of them has ever written a palindrome without a mispelling here or there. Liqueurs work better: *Evolution: dog, otter, a man on amaretto—God? No. I tu love.*

Orphan? Nah. Pro.

Is it I? Hi! 'Tis I, Oliver said, in introducing himself to Fagin. Fagin wondered, *Oliver evil? O!* Then replied, *Spare me raps.*

OLIVER TWIST PALINDROME

MELBA IS TOAST PALINDROME

Ahem, a doable Melba, Nellie, mad, amiable Melba—I'm a Dame. I'll enable Melba? O Dame? Ha!

To Melba toast! It's a—O—table mot! is the standard Pythonian expression while breaking bread.

Red underpants. A last nap. Red! Nuder!

Sounds like a plan. Nevertheless, the prudent course in addressing a masseuse might well include *Ahem! No leg gel on me, ha!*

STRIPPER'S WISH LIST PALINDROME

Mood is all as I do Om.

When Palin got the call from McCartney in India describing the problems the Beatles were having with their meditationalist, Evan, Paul put him on the phone, screaming, *"Navel, Evan!"* Evan's reply: *"Maharishi Jijih, sir, a ham."*

MEDITATION PALINDROME

Nada martinis in it: Ramadan.

Eurobar, Arab, O rue!

EAST MEETS WEST PALINDROME

JOSEPHINE'S PALINDROME

Revolts el Bonaparte. He trap a noblest lover.

The luckiest palindromic discovery was the simple translation of Napoleon's famous remark on debarking on *Elba: Capable* j'etais avant que j'ai vu Elbe. This became *Able was I ere I saw Elba*. Of course, if he had taken the trouble to learn English, he may well have devised: *Napoleon's Nöel! O Pan!* as a Christmas greeting, or *Sit! Is Noel! O pang! Napoleons it is!* for introducing the dessert menu.

Tulsa slut as a Tulsa slut.

Strips? Peels? O temerity—as to peep at a—rue, yo voyeur!—at a pee pot, say. Tire me to sleep, spir'ts. For the aspiring thespian, a subtler sobriquet might be *A ham of Omaha*. Of course, if you're a dog—well, Lassie once barked, *Fra? Rot. Cat actor. Arf!*

TYPECASTING PALINDROME

Borrow, or rob?

If the latter, one could *Rob a Gabor.* Of course, that might set off *a moral aroma.* Either way, it pays to be thinking: *No, sir. Pay all. Allay a prison.*

ETHICAL DILEMMA PALINDROME

BUREAUCRACY PALINDROME

Loco torpor, or, O protocol!

Warren Harding exclaimed, on exiting the White House hung-over, *"Sun? O blare de federal bonus!"* Calvin Coolidge has been described as *Lackluster. Fret, sulk, Cal.* When Ike took office, he opined, *"CIA: some mosaic!"* Then *"Ten I back: cabinet."* Jimmy Carter once bragged, *I made Ron, pal, foil Gorb., M., in an imbroglio flap. No Red am I.* Nixon's secret tapes speak of a *"cam o' top Potomac."*

EVERYTHING'S RELATIVE PALINDROME

To Idi Amin I'm a idiot.

I diminish sin? I'm Idi! = Idiocy c/o Idi.

About the Author

Fired from Hallmark for writing meaningful greeting-card verse, he once ran twenty straight balls at pool; finished 183rd (out of about 10,000) at the 1985 U.S. Open Crossword Puzzle Tournament; won a yodeling contest in a German restaurant; was bitten by a guard dog in a tattoo parlor; survived a car crash with Sidney Lumet; Paul Newman once claimed to have known him for a long time; has not been arrested in 17 months. He is the author of *A Boilermaker for the Lady* (NYQ Books).

About the Illustrator

A celebrity comic book artist in France, Philippe Petit-Roulet is known best in the US for his New Yorker covers and spots. He has published half a dozen comic books with Didier Martiny, and many books, including *Spots,* Editions Cornelius (2014), *Precis d'architecture* (2012) and *Les Bras de Morphee* (2010) both with Alain Beaulet; as well as *Music Is* with Lloyd Moss, published in the US by Penguin Putnam in 2003. He has participated in advertising campaigns worldwide, and received awards for his playful graphic drawings and animations from Communications Arts in America, Art Directors' Club in France, and the Bradford Animation Festival in England. He lives in Paris with his wife and children.

The New York Quarterly Foundation, Inc.
New York, New York

Poetry Magazine
Since 1969

Edgy, fresh, groundbreaking, eclectic—voices from all walks of life.

Definitely NOT your mama's poetry magazine!

The *New York Quarterly* has been defining the term contemporary American poetry since its first craft interview with W. H. Auden.

Interviews • Essays • and of course, lots of poems.

www.nyq.org

No contest! That's correct, NYQ Books are NO CONTEST to other small presses because we do not support ourselves through contests. Our books are carefully selected by invitation only, so you know that NYQ Books are produced with the same editorial integrity as the magazine that has brought you the most eclectic contemporary American poetry since 1969.

Books

www.nyq.org

poetry at the edge™

www.ingramcontent.com/pod-product-compliance
Lightning Source LLC
LaVergne TN
LVHW020937090426
835512LV00020B/3400